AUSTRALIAN WILDLIFE

THE SHOCKING TRUTH!

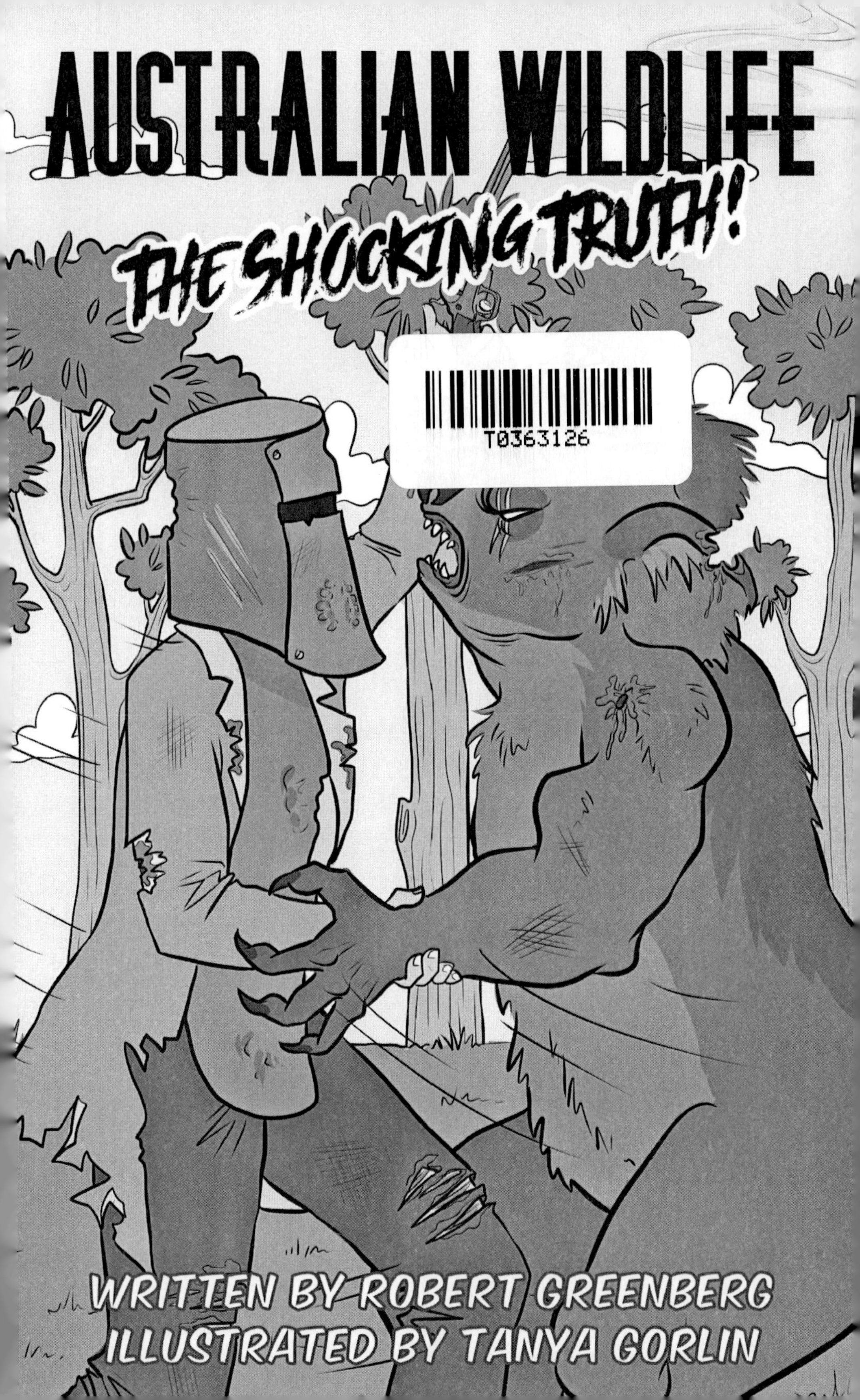

WRITTEN BY ROBERT GREENBERG
ILLUSTRATED BY TANYA GORLIN

DISCLAIMER

AUSTRALIAN WILDLIFE
THE SHOCKING TRUTH!

written by Robert Greenberg
illustrated by Tanya Gorlin

Published by:
Boolarong Press
38/1631 Wynnum Road
Tingalpa Qld 4173
Australia.
www.boolarongpress.com.au

First published 2020

 A catalogue record for this book is available from the National Library of Australia

ISBN: 9781925877410 (paperback)

Typeset by Boolarong Press in Raleway 11pt

Cover artwork by Tanya Gorlin

Edited by Wordwright, www.wordwrightediting.com.au.

Printed and bound by Watson Ferguson & Company, Tingalpa, Australia

Contents

Introduction

I shall be blunt and get immediately to the point!

For too many years, successive Australian governments have wilfully and consistently conspired to deceive the world by covering up the true, vile nature of much of Australia's flora and fauna!

Yes, we have always freely admitted to having a few of Mother Nature's greatest villains in our midst: the ferocious great white shark, the deadly saltwater crocodile, the venomous taipan and box jellyfish just to name a few. However, over the years, consecutive governments have never dared come clean to the full extent of the terrors that swarm and thrive among us for fear of frightening away potential migrants and capital investment.

The seemingly sweet and cuddly marsupials, our garrulous and colourful bird life, the strange and exotic monotremes, reptiles, plant life and insectoid residents of our great southern land have all received many a plaudit from all corners of the globe. But never before has the deceitful veil of secrecy been lifted as to their true violent and lude natures until today; for we are not only a land of wonders, but of monsters as well!

Despite our stoic good humour, we are a nation besieged, for almost every living thing in our great brown land is aggressive toward us!

The simple truth is this — much of Australian wildlife's feeding and breeding habits are not only unique to our continent, but often totally hostile to humankind in every way. Although many might look sweet and innocent, most Australian beasts are carnivorous by nature and vicious by choice! Whether it grows, swims, flies, crawls, slithers, hops or glides etc., it will either kill you; kill you then eat you; "violate" you, kill you then eat you; or just settle for laying its eggs in your brain!

Now, for the first time ever, this despicable cover-up will be exposed, the whistle blown, and the shocking TRUTH finally revealed!

Be it known that Australian Parks and Wildlife Services and Tourism Australia have not approved this book ...

Robert Greenberg

How to Enjoy Your Australian Holiday

Visiting Australia need not be considered a threat to life and limb, just as long as you take a few very simple precautions and follow a few basic rules that will ensure your stay is a safe, happy and memorable one.

1. For peace of mind, have all your life, health and funeral insurance fully paid up.

2. Australia has the most venomous animals, insects and plants in the world, so all visitors should be fully vaccinated before leaving home or at least avail themselves of the broad spectrum antivenene freely available from the airport, schools, hospitals, medical centres, post offices, and fire and police stations, and in any home or office first aid cabinet. This simple, one-shot inoculation is for your wellbeing, and a yearly vaccination is essential for all citizens and long-term visitors. Remember, to go unvaccinated is to court disaster!

Fun fact: Vegemite, Australia's favourite family spread, was invented by the first Australians. It was discovered that a thick paste made from black beetles, dirt and wallaby droppings makes an excellent repellent, as its robust taste and smell tend to make those who regularly eat it unpalatable to most predators. This puts them "off the bite", so Vegemite has always been considered an effective and trusted natural antivenene, repellent and general "cure all" to this day.

3. Always stay in authorised "safe zones" at all times.

4. When in the bush, keep your wits about you, stay in a group at all times and NEVER walk alone or stray off the path, even if you desperately feel nature's call and need to spray

the Australian countryside with a deft hand and a flick of the wrist. You could so easily be picked off by any number of beasts!

Remember all bush tracks are well defined and patrolled. Additionally, every 200 metres or so there will be a safety shelter with a solid lockable door, stocks of antivenene and a panic button.

However, many still venture foolishly into the scrub alone against all common sense and advice and have never been seen or heard from again.

If you desperately want to venture into the wilds, always go in numbers and with an accredited and experienced armed guide.

5. Keep in mind that suburban parks and sporting venues etc. could also be dangerous to the unwary. Even the average backyard can prove to be a quarter-acre deathtrap.

6. Above all, try not to worry too much and HAVE FUN!

THE SULPHUR CRESTED COCKATOO AND OTHER PARROTS

A noisy and obnoxious creature at the best of times, this feathered fiend becomes particularly nasty, if not downright dangerous, during its mating season around August to January when it goes on the hunt for fresh meat to feed its hatchlings — a habit shared by almost all other large species of parrot that reside in Australia. The sulphur-crested breed, however, is the most well-known for its cunning and aggression.

Small children and tots in prams are particularly vulnerable to this winged predator, who will swoop down from the branches screeching loudly to startle the child's parent, then nip off a finger or toe before swiftly ascending back to its nesting tree!

A sulphur crested cockatoo feeding its young their favourite treat.

THE COCKATIEL

The cockatiel might look similar to a delightful character from a popular Japanese children's cartoon series, but that's where the resemblance ends. Without a doubt, the cockatiel has got to be the most obnoxious, moronic and loutish of all Australian animals, a real flock of hoons and yobbos!

During the mating season, they readily demonstrate their "bogan" side by defending their roosting trees with such oafish aggression that they have even put the mighty koala and insidious brushtail possum to flight!

In fact, the first illustrator of this book got too close to a group of broody cockatiels and, well, he should have known better ...!

"Hoons", "yobbos" and "bogans" are an obnoxious, moronic and loutish species of Australian of the two-legged variety.

The usual suspects, cute little birds with a "gansta" attitude!

THE MAGPIE

Like so many Australian animals, the magpie is a Jekyll and Hyde.

For most of the year, the birds are fairly laid-back and inoffensive creatures, and their warblings each morning and evening as they salute and farewell the sun are a welcome part of Aussie suburban life. However, come spring when the large mature birds' mating season begins, they become highly aggressive and territorial and will fiercely defend their nesting trees. During this period, their calls strike terror into all who hear them!

Younger, smaller magpies are content to mostly laze about the suburbs, typically feeding on grubs and lizards. However, as they mature, these magpies spread their wings (which can span as much as two metres) and seek the open spaces of the countryside and their tastes turn to larger game. This is usually not of concern to the human population, with these larger birds preferring to go after rabbits, bush pigs and the odd sheep or two.

However, in the mating season when their testosterone is at its peak, the magpies become emboldened, and while the younger birds content themselves with merely swooping and pecking at people, the big adults will often put household pets and even small children on the menu.

The shadow of a magpie, terror of the preschool!

THE SUPERB FAIRY-WREN & WILLIE WAGTAIL

These small and seemingly innocuous birds that inhabit most parts of south-eastern Australia are the real Jekyll and Hyde of our suburban skies. Some will become attached to people and follow them around for a day or two, singing merrily and hopping about in a friendly manner. However, without warning or provocation, they will suddenly attack — pecking and scratching wildly at the victim's face while screeching horribly. This onslaught will continue until the bird is finally killed or disabled.

The birds can do minimal physical damage, but the shock value of their assault is highly unsettling.

THE EMU

Capable of running the best part of 90 kilometres/hour (55 miles/hour) and standing a good 3 metres (9 feet), emus are probably the most ferocious and cunning of all Australian birdlife. They are best avoided at all cost as, like so many of Australia's wildlife, they are carnivorous by nature and vicious by choice. In 1932, we even went to war against them, all to no avail and at great cost to human life! Of course, they are still considered a valuable natural commodity and hunted to this day for their fine oil, pelts and feathers by highly skilled hunters in armoured 4WDs.

Beware the great Australian land shark!

THE CASSOWARY

Whereas the emu can be found in the verdant plains of our continent, the cassowary is mostly encountered haunting our northern rainforests. Although it shares the same vicious nature of its larger cousin, the cassowary comes far better equipped. Its armoury not only includes size, speed and sharp teeth, but a rapier-like middle toe that can disembowel with a single swipe, as well as a battering ram crest on its head that can dent even the toughest armour plate, let alone a human skull.

In her informative 1953 book Vindictive Birds of Australasia, the renowned ornithologist Evelyn Sylvia Isaac Greenfield wrote:

> The inner of its three toes is fitted with a long, straight, murderous talon which can sever an arm or eviscerate an abdomen with the greatest of ease as well as a tough, bony, skin-covered "helmet" on their heads that is often used as a lethal bludgeon. There are many records of natives being killed by this wantonly homicidal bird!

During World War II, American and Australian troops training in the Top End were warned to steer well clear of them at all costs as they were considered even more ferocious than the Japanese at close quarters.

Beware the mighty cassowary, the "velociraptor" of the rainforest!

THE FAIRY PENGUIN

Fast and agile swimmers with excellent senses both above and below the waves, there is nothing remotely "fairy" about these feathered predators. They will attack, kill and devour *en masse* anything that blunders into their territory no matter the size. Just like the Amazonian piranha, even a small shoal of them can reduce an unwary swimmer down to the bare bone within minutes.

It is very rare to survive a fairy penguin attack.

THE LYREBIRD

Unlike the whipbird that can produce a cry so loud it can induce deafness and even neurological damage to those unfortunate to blunder into its nesting site, the lyrebird will mimic almost anything it hears, and will often reproduce the sound of predators to protect its nesting site from intruders.

However, for reasons unknown, the lyrebird has been known to stealthily follow bushwalkers while making the sounds of enraged koalas and other fearsome creatures, normally sending the bushwalkers running in blind panic. Experts suggest that the bird does this for the mere vindictive fun of it.

A lyrebird mimicking the call of some Australia's most dangerous beasts. >>

THE BRUSH TURKEY

The brush turkey appears to be an innocuous sort of a bird at first, inoffensively wandering around the forest floor raking over leaf litter looking for grubs, seeds and fallen fruits to eat. However, looks can be deceiving, for like most Australian wildlife, this bird is venomous and its venom is one of the most unusual and lethal in all the animal kingdom!

During the mating season from August to December, the males go on the hunt, not only for a mate, but for fresh meat for the females to lay their eggs upon. The male turkey's feet have four strong gripping claws, the rear one of which secretes a slow acting neurotoxin. When on the hunt, the bird cautiously stalks through the undergrowth and, on finding a suitable victim (usually a wallaby, goanna, feral cat or stray bushwalker), attacks by suddenly darting out of the scrub and slashing viciously with its rear claw before rapidly dashing back into cover.

It has been reported by the few survivors of a brush turkey attack that at first there is a pleasant narcotic effect from the neurotoxin, which creates a sense of euphoria and disconnection with reality. This makes the victims stumble aimlessly and happily about for an hour or two until they eventually succumb to sudden cardiac and pulmonary arrest. Once down, the bird moves in and begins to build a large nest of heaped up leaves over the body. When this is done, a succession of local females will gradually arrive for mating and egg-laying. Not only does the decaying flesh keep the eggs warm during their seven-week incubation period, it also provides the chicks with their first meal once they have hatched.

A male brush turkey completing its nest before mating.

THE BUDGIE AND THE BROLGA

Like so many creatures that inhabit our land, the budgerigar, or "budgie", is yet another Jekyll and Hyde. Although they make wonderful pets and spend most of their time chirping happily away to themselves while innocently nibbling away at a wide variety of seeds, fruits and berries, come breeding season when there are younglings to feed and territory to be defended, our sweet little budgies becomes blood-crazed flying piranhas of the air, swarming and darkening the southern skies in their insatiable hunt for flesh!

The brolga is another dangerous Australian bird. The male brolga is probably the most territorial of Australian birds and will defend its nesting sites with almost suicidal tenacity. Keen of eye and swift of wing, they attack by diving into their victims at speeds of up to 110 kilometres/hour, skewering them through and through with deadly accuracy!

After a few weeks, when the body has decomposed from the tropical heat, the brolga will use the victim's remains in an obscene mating dance, tossing bones high into the air to showcase to prospective mates its hunting and killing prowess.

Upper picture: There is nothing more terrifying than a blizzard of crazed carnivorous budgies out for blood!

Lower picture: A brolga skewering an unfortunate victim and its grotesque mating dance. >>

THE KOOKABURRA

The jolly, garrulous, laughing kookaburra has long been a favourite icon and mainstay of the Australian tourism industry. However, they also have an unfortunate fondness for eyeballs and a sarcastic cackle that strikes fear into all who hear it!

If you think that long beak of theirs is just for catching lizards and grasshoppers, you will be mistaken!

THE GOLDEN ORB WEAVER AND AUSTRALIAN JUMPING SPIDERS

Most Australian spiders can grow to an enormous size and can spin huge webs. As an example, the golden orb weaver grows to almost 2 metres in length measured from its fangs to the tip of its abdomen, and can spin a web so strong it can even ensnare the mighty koala.

There are many species of Australian jumping spider, and many can grow to be as large as cats and launch themselves a full 25 metres to attack their prey. They are found in all parts of Australia, including the cities and suburbs.

Upper picture: A golden orb weaver in mortal combat!
Lower picture: An Australian jumping
spider attacking a pedestrian.

25

THE REDBACK SPIDER

Small, venomous, aggressively territorial and agile, with a strange attraction to bathrooms and the underside of toilet seats, the redback spider has been celebrated in story, verse and song since it was first painfully discovered by the early settlers.

Normally a glossy black in colour with a distinctive bright red stripe on its abdomen, the redback spider is, in fact, a chameleon-like master of disguise that can blend into almost any environment. As such, every visit to an Australian bathroom is always a nerve-racking adventure …

There are 23 of these little buggers hiding in this one suburban toilet. See if you can spot them all!

The Daddy Long-Legs and Huntsman Spider

The South American wandering spider (also known as the banana spider) has a frightening reputation for aggression and a venom that causes prolonged "priapism" (prolonged erection) in human males before a painful and lingering death. Fortunately, the venom from its Australian relative, the daddy-long-legs, shares only one of these traits in that it's capable of keeping the most disinterested and slovenly of "soldiers" standing rigidly to attention for hours without the fatal side effects.

Waggishly christened "walking viagra" or the "daddy-long-shlong" by the Australian population, the daddy-long-legs has been a welcome if not mischievous part of Australian life since the first man and woman set foot on the continent eons ago.

However, despite widespread affection by the Australian population, extremist religious groups have long waged a relentless holy war against this naughty little arachnid, claiming it's the root cause of all our nation's woes from the moral decay of the population to the onset of drought and flood. Due to this mindset, they have relentlessly lobbied successive governments over the years for a national eradication program. Thankfully, this has been to no avail.

Australia is also home to the fearsome huntsman spider! Many times more dangerous than the funnel-web and redback that grab all the headlines, this large, cunning and aggressive spider likes to inhabit unkempt gardens and derelict buildings and is a real threat to the careless and unwary.

The huntsman spider is most active at night, leaving their lairs and creeping through the dark, dimly lit parks, backstreets and gardens of suburbia in search of prey, always keeping to the shadows till they are ready to strike. Usually an ambush hunter, the huntsman spider will still readily creep into suburban dwellings in search of easy pickings.

Not all things that go "bump" in the night are welcome ones ...

THE FUNNEL-WEB SPIDER

The funnel-web spider has always been the Jekyll and Hyde of Australian arachnids. It is very large (although smaller than other Australian species), very ugly, highly venomous and sometimes aggressive. However, it also possess one of the sweetest and most melodic singing voices of the entire insect kingdom, and is generally jolly and good-natured when not busy killing something.

It's a real treat hearing them every spring and summer morning, singing away joyfully from the tops of fences and roofs across suburbia, greeting the sun with their light-hearted tunes before scurrying away back to their cosy burrows. You can also often hear them warbling a merry little refrain to themselves as they carry off someone's cat or schnauzer (its favourite treat) down into their lair.

It's hard not to love them!

There are 40 different species of funnel-web spider, including the Bankstown Blue, Southern Fluffy, Melbourne Green Silky, Royal Northern Tiger and Red-banded Jumping Goliath, as well as a wide variety of "boutique" hybrids like the Gorgeous Baboon and the very popular Springer Roughie and Hungry Mo, to name but a few.

Most breeds can be domesticated after a fashion, and the display hosted by the Australian Funnel-web Breeders Society at the Sydney Royal Easter Show is always well attended, with the petting zoo being a popular Easter treat for kiddies of all ages. However, due to some unfortunate past experiences, the event is always scheduled so it doesn't coincide with important dog, cat or reptile shows ...

*In this image we have Mrs Mary Pock of
Narrabeen on Sydney's beautiful Northern
Beaches receiving the Grand Champion's prize
at the 2019 Australasian nationals with her famous purebred
Sydney Black, "Harold", named after her late husband.
Mrs Pock has also lost three cats and two dogs to her hobby,
but as she says with a twinkle in her eye, "Why just have two or
four legs scuttling about the house when you can enjoy eight!"*

MOTHS AND BUTTERFLIES

Australian moths and butterflies are some of the most beautiful and exotic in the world, and of course, some of them are thoroughly unpleasant!

The average Australian caterpillar is covered with very fine little hairs that, when brushed against, will lodge in your skin, usually causing only mild irritation. Unfortunately, in some of our species, notably the Bogon, Tiger, Leaf Roller and Bell moths, as well as the Cairns Birdwing, Red-banded Jezebel and Purple Copper butterflies, these fine little hairs are in fact its eggs.

Just like the South American botfly, the grubs cocoon themselves just underneath a victim's skin and feed on the host's blood until finally pupating and eventually hatching out as adult moths and butterflies a week or two later.

Unpleasant as it is, contact with these insects usually poses no real threat for a fit and healthy person who has been inoculated or can reach medical attention.

Anyone who has been in contact with a caterpillar of any species should get to a doctor or pest exterminator as soon as possible, or at least spray themselves with insecticide before the grubs hatch.

THE BUSH TICK

The Australian bush tick is a vile little beast. Not only will its venom kill most house pets and make the most robust person rapidly sick for days, it will also lay its eggs in the same wound it feeds from. Many people never know they are an incubator for these insect bloodsuckers until the hatchlings erupt from under their skin. This usually happens in the dead of night while the victim sleeps, with the hatchlings continuing to feed on their unaware host.

Those who are old, sick, not inoculated or cannot receive immediate medical attention are in real danger of severe blood loss, with several deaths a year commonplace among this unfortunate segment of the population.

*Those venturing into the bush should always be vaccinated or,
at the very least, wear one of the readily available tick collars.*

The Millipede and Centipede

Australian millipedes and centipedes are, of course, the largest and most lethal found anywhere in the world.

Both species are fairly similar, growing on average between 7 and 10 metres in length when fully matured. They can be found in almost all woodlands and forests throughout Australia, and are both incredibly active and ferocious hunters.

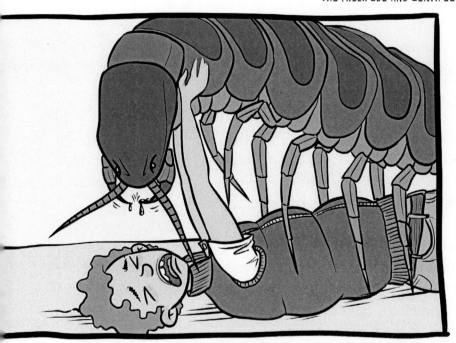

The centipede kills by biting with its powerful and venomous jaws, while the millipede kills by constricting, strangling and crushing its victims to death. That's how you can tell the difference between the two.

THE CICADA

The vast majority of cicadas are a welcome, if not noisy addition to every Australian summer. Most, such as the Green Grocer, Golden Twanger and Cherrynose, are benign in their habits, and their lightly roasted larval casings have always been a favourite children's Christmas treat.

However, there are always a few fearsome and rotten apples in every Australian barrel, such as the Masked Devil, Southern Red-eyed Squeaker and the big Double Drummer. These brutes are particularly nasty, as they not only possess formidable mandibles, long, sharp, hooked legs and paralysis-inducing stingers, but also have particularly unpleasant breeding habits!

Unlike their harmless cousins, the dangerous varieties of cicada are nearly always silent, that is, until the moment they attack! A cicada's attack is "pure precision in insect form". The beast flies silently and cautiously, with its long legs tucked up under its body. Upon seeing a likely host, the cicada will spread them wide and, on landing, arch its head and abdomen back, screeching loudly and opening its mandibles before raising its stinger. If there is no response from its target, it will soon release and fly away. However, if there is a reaction, it will bite down with its jaws and drive its stinger into the victim. Those who have been attacked will tell you the sting itself is not particularly painful, but its bite is excruciating and its high-pitched screech is both frightening and deafening!

Once the prospective host is rendered immobile by the venom, the cicada will use its proboscis to inject three to four eggs under the skin.

The parasitic cicada larva will slowly move through the body, feeding on the host's blood until they come to rest in order to pupate. This usually occurs in the joints and neck. After three to four weeks, they will erupt from under the skin and fly away to continue the breeding cycle.

A cicada making its approach ...

BULL ANTS

There are approximately 1300+ species of ant in Australia, of which there are 90 or so species of bull ant.

Australian bull ants grow to about 40 millimetres in length and can be found throughout the continent. They all have powerful jaws and nasty stingers in their abdomen, excellent eyesight, and most have the ability to jump up to a metre when attacking and are, of course, are highly aggressive.

The undisputed king of all Australian bull ants is the mighty Giant Red, also known as the Bull-Jo or Red Bulldog. These brutes can be found in the tropics and semi-arid parts of Australia and can grow to as much as 18+ centimetres in length!

As well as having the attributes already mentioned above, they also seem to be quite intelligent, and make a highly unsettling ticking and chirping sound as they click their long mandibles together in what entomologists theorise is a rudimentary form of communication not unlike dolphins …

Another feature of this species is that they let out a disturbing, high-pitched "death squeal" if injured, which alerts others to come to their aid in a rapid, overwhelming and swarming attack.

Take on one, take on all!

41

MOSQUITOES

There are about 300 species of mosquitoes in Australia. Only a handful of them are benign, while almost all others spread deadly disease such as Murray Valley encephalitis, Ross River and Barmah Forest viruses, as well as dengue fever to name but a few.

FLIES

There are approximately 30,000+ species of fly in Australia, some big some small, but all of them quite fearless.

Not much more needs to be said really.

Though most mosquito species are small, others are large and dangerously predatory, and as for flies, not much more needs to be said really.

THE PAPER WASP

The average Australian paper wasp has a wingspan of up to 30 centimetres, and is capable of carrying off small cats and dogs to feed its young.

Although an aggressive and frightening-looking insect with a vicious sting, they are highly susceptible to any common household insecticide or tennis racquet ...

And poor Mr Fluffy Bum was never seen or heard from again.

SCORPIONS

Found throughout Australia, the average scorpion only grows to about 15–20 centimetres in length, and fortunately is usually shy and wary of humans. However, in the deep interior deserts, this insect can grow close to 8 metres in length or more, and can pose a serious threat to all who encounter it!

Desert homesteads are always solidly constructed with strong walls and fences, and any landholder would be foolish to venture out unarmed!

Its only known enemy is the mighty thorny devil, a reptile of almost dinosaur proportions. When these two beasts meet, you can be assured that a spectacular and terrifying battle will ensue!

A scorpion and thorny devil battling to secure territory.

SNAKES

Australian snakes, as can be expected, are more aggressive and venomous than any others found throughout the world, and usually grow anywhere between 10 and 40 metres in length. These carnivorous reptiles happily eat rottweilers, cattle and even people like popcorn.

A rare image of an Australian snake on the hunt and stalking its prey.

FRILL-NECKED LIZARD

Not particularly dangerous or even overly aggressive when young, frill-necked lizards are more of a nuisance, as they will incessantly follow you around all day hissing noisily, and jumping up and down while displaying their frills in an attempt to scare you with their "frightening" display.

While this display can be considered cute and almost endearing during a frill-neck's early years, upon getting older and larger, the lizard easily gains the ability to rip a victim's head off with just one bite.

Almost cute in an obnoxious sort of way, that's unless their larger siblings decide to show up ... >>

THE FRESH WATER TURTLE

The Australian freshwater turtle has always been the stuff of legend and the inspiration for most of the lurid and fanciful tales of our mythical water monster, the bunyip. The real beast, however, is of course far more lethal than any fairytale creature could ever be.

Measuring about 4 to 5 metres across its shell and possessing a long, sinuous, muscular neck of almost 7 metres in length, ending with a wide gaping mouth with powerful, distensible jaws, coupled with sharp eyesight and a keen sense of smell, this creature is yet another feared predator of our inland waterways.

The brute silently glides just below the water's surface along the edge of billabongs, creeks and rivers in search of prey, with only the tip of its nose barely above the surface, testing the air for any scent of possible quarry. When it detects a likely target, it then uses its keen eyesight, and stealthily moves in for the kill.

The turtle strikes like lightning, with its long neck exploding out of the water, engulfing its unwary prey within its muscular jaws. Gripped tight with no way of escape, the victim is then dragged into the waters' depths to be swallowed whole.

*A turtle dragging yet another victim beneath
the waters for consumption.*

THE BLUE-TONGUE LIZARD

Though venomous like most creatures that inhabit our continent, the blue-tongue lizard is not aggressive or territorial in any way, and is probably the most laid-back, gentle and relaxed of all Australian fauna.

However, if roughly handled or frightened, they can be roused to defend themselves.

If bitten, the blue-tongue's venom is promptly absorbed through the skin, and though not deadly, it is a potent hallucinogenic that rapidly renders any attacker "happily" insensible for several hours.

For this reason, the blue-tongue lizard was often used by our first Australians in their dreaming ceremonies to produce wonderful and vivid visions.

During the 1800s, refined and diluted venom was sold as a sedative and general cure-all. However, overuse was found to lead to lifelong addiction, causing it to be removed from sale in the early 1920s.

Accidentally (or intentionally) tripping merrily away in the bush could see you fall prey to any number of unfriendly beasts, all too willing to kill your buzz. >>

GOANNA

Masters of camouflage and growing to about 3 to 5 metres in length, these sinuous beasts are the most cunning hunters in Australia, found lurking in all parts of the country.

Similar to the octopus and cuttlefish, almost all species of this reptile can not only change their colour at will, but also alter their body shape to produce spikes, bumps or frills, allowing them to completely blend into their surroundings.

The goanna is intelligent, mildly venomous, and reasonably fast over short distances. Additionally, goannas possess an acute sense of smell, which makes them excellent trackers and drug/bomb detection tools, with the smaller, more easily trained species being deployed by police and customs officers since the 1960s.

Police goannas are a common site at Australian airports.

THE GIANT GIPPSLAND EARTHWORM

These magnificent subterranean beasts can grow to almost 20 metres (65 feet) in length and almost 1 metre (3 feet) in girth. Though they subsist mostly on carrion, they are capable of dragging sheep and even small cattle, as well as unwary farmers, down to their doom!

In recent decades, the tables have turned on these majestic predators of the underworld. The vast herds that once roamed abundant in all parts of subterranean rural Victoria and the Latrobe Valley have now been dramatically thinned. This is due to over-hunting and poaching, as their flesh is delicious and of remarkable quality, having a uniquely sweet yet robustly gamey taste. They are now a protected species, similar to the great white shark.

Commercial farming has been attempted since the mid-1980s with little success. However, research continues and a farming breakthrough may just be around the corner …

It is said that during moonlit nights, the great worm rises from the earth to feed.

THE BEACH WORM

These worms can be found burrowed in sandy areas throughout the south-eastern coast of Australia at the low water mark, and are popular as fishing bait. They also share the same highly unpleasant trait of the infamous candiru, or "vampire fish", of the Amazon basin in that they will attempt to enter any body cavity in an effort to lay their eggs and then feed from the inside out ...

Though attacks are rare, "skinny dipping" on the east coast of Australia is definitely not recommended. In case of an attack, the only course of action is to find the closest fisherman who knows how to use a stink bag and hand bait to try to lure them out, or someone who's handy with a yabby pump ...

Never get drunk and try to sleep it off at the beach.

The blue swimmer and mud crabs

When young, the blue swimmer crab has a nasty habit of swimming up under seagulls paddling about on the surface, grabbing a leg and feeding on it. This is why it's not uncommon to see one-legged seagulls hobbling about on Australian beaches. When they reach adulthood and measure a good metre or more across the carapace, blue swimmer crabs go after bigger game and prefer to stalk unweary surfers, bodyboarders and wading fishermen ...

The Australian mud crab, on the other hand, is found in mangrove swamps and mudflats throughout the continent. It is little more than an aquatic "tank" that can measure as much as 2 to 3 metres across its carapace, and comes armed with pincers that can generate up to 30 tonnes of crushing force. In the northern parts of the country, their favourite treats are saltwater crocodiles and bull sharks.

During WWII, a Japanese reconnaissance party of 25 highly trained and heavily armed marines attempted to come ashore through the mangroves just outside Broome in Western Australia. Scouting for suitable landing sites for a full amphibious invasion of the Top End, they were never seen or heard from again ...

The only good thing is, they both taste delicious! >>

63

THE BLUE-RINGED OCTOPUS

Cute, shy and innocent-looking, so small and petite it can snuggle into a bottle cap, its bite is so venomous it can kill 40 full-grown men with just one little nip!

Whereas most lethal animals in Australia grow to enormous dimensions, the little blue-ringed octopus can kill just as easily, and is only a hundredth of the size.

THE MULLET

For the most part, mullet are harmless enough. Yes, their schools have been known to attack unwary swimmers, but due to their lack of any real teeth, they can do little harm. However, a few in every five thousand or so will metamorphose to become one of the legendary beasts of the Australasian deep — the great southern oceanic mullet!

The great oceanic mullet is the undisputed monarch of the Australasian depths and grows to at least 35 metres in length. It is believed that specimens over 50 metres could be lurking in the abyssal deep off the continental shelf and they could well have life spans of hundreds of years! They range widely throughout the world's oceans and have been found from the North Pole to the South. However, they are most common in our southern seas.

The great oceanic mullet is not known to be overly aggressive or even an active predator, but more an opportunistic one that will engulf anything that comes within range of its cavernous mouth, which can measure between 8 and 10 metres across! Dolphins, sharks, giant squid and even juvenile great oceanic mullet have all been discovered in its vast stomach, as well as a few unfortunate seamen and deep-sea divers.

HAZARDS OF THE 1836 GREAT MULLET FISHERY

In years gone by, the southern white whale was the usual target of whalers. However, if the cry, "Mullet ho!" was heard, all thought of perusing mere mammals was put on hold as a far greater (and more dangerous) prize was in the offering, as this early woodcut, "Hazards of the 1836 Great Mullet fishery", will attest.

LANTANA

When first introduced to Australia in 1841, the lantana was nothing more than an innocuous ornamental garden plant. However, by the 1860s, it had naturalised and mutated into the dangerous noxious weed we have today!

All parts of the lantana are highly toxic, and in the humid summer months, the creeping lantana grows voraciously, with the capability of inundating an entire township almost overnight. It is a constant battle in Australia to keep the weed at bay, with some smaller towns being lost forever.

The only way to control the lantana is by cutting it off at its main root, a task fraught with danger, for many have entered a thicket never to be seen or heard from again ...

The tragic 1975 overnight inundation of Onagawoopwoop.

THE GYMPIE GYMPIE

The Gympie Gympie, also known as the "giant stinging tree", "stinging brush", "mulberry-leaved stinger" and the "suicide plant", is a particularly sinister member of the nettle family with a nasty surprise for anyone that stumbles across it in Australia's northern rainforests.

The entire plant is covered with fine, hollow stinging hairs that if merely brushed against will deliver a potent neurotoxin that will induce an agonising pain so severe that it has been described as "being burnt with hot acid and electrocuted at the same time". This is followed by a continuous painful torment and an allergic reaction that may last for weeks or even years if all the hairs are not immediately removed from the victim's body.

There are numerous reports of pack horses going mad and jumping in agony off cliffs; forestry workers drinking themselves into oblivion trying to dull the pain; as well soldiers who were undergoing jungle training needing to be strapped down to hospital beds and heavily sedated for days on end due to the horrific painful effects of this plant. There was even one terrible case of a poor officer shooting himself after using a leaf for "toilet purposes".

It is strongly recommended that people visiting our northern rainforests wear protective clothing at all times and take antihistamine tablets in advance to avoid the horrible consequences of brushing against a Gympie Gympie!

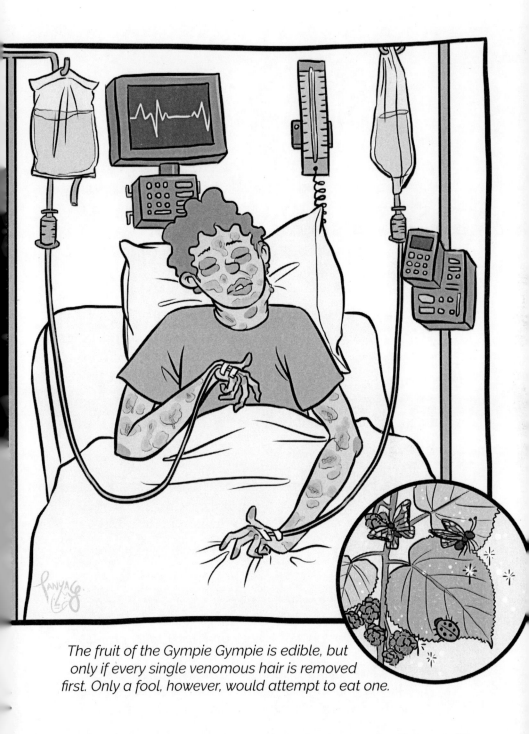

The fruit of the Gympie Gympie is edible, but only if every single venomous hair is removed first. Only a fool, however, would attempt to eat one.

THE BANKSIA TREE

Bushfires are a common and essential part of the Australian ecosystem, with many plants and animals adapting to take advantage of this regular, natural event. Numerous species of reptile eggs and plant seeds will not hatch or germinate until they have been washed over by life-giving fire.

Every bushfire season, our brave fire fighters put their lives on the line to protect their fellow Australians' lives and property. However, it's not just the heat, smoke and flame they must be wary of, but the lethal seed pods of the banksia tree as well.

The banksia has a unique and lethal way of spreading its seeds. During the height of a fire, the core of its seed pods heats up to tremendous pressures until they violently rupture with a resounding bang, scattering seeds with deadly force in all directions for a distance of up to 10 metres!

Upper picture: Many fire fronts throughout the land often sound like war zones, with fire fighters always being clothed in fire-retardant flack vests and helmets for protection.

Lower picture: During WWI, the Anzacs were armed with banksia seed pods dipped in flammable tar until reliable hand grenades could be deployed.. >>

THE WARATAH

The waratah can grow to weigh as much as a tonne and is the largest, most voracious of all the world's carnivorous plants, with long, highly sensitive, sinewy creepers that spread out in all directions from the main "flower", which can grow to a length of over 50 metres. These muscular tendrils can lie passively in wait or actively seek out prey to feed their enormous appetites.

It also emits powerful and enticing pheromones that are irresistible to almost all animals and insects, and draws them in from kilometres around to meet their eventual doom.

Once caught, few ever escape. >>

THE WATTLE TREE

For all its iconic beauty and sweet benign looks, the wattle is the most insidious and feared of all Australian plants, even more so than the terrifying waratah!

The wattle earns its sinister reputation through its similarity to the *Ophiocordyceps* genus of fungi known as the "zombie ant fungus".

Ophiocordyceps are mostly found in the tropical forests of Thailand and Brazil, and gets its "undead" nickname due to its ability to alter its ant victims' behaviour.

Once an ant's brain is infected by an *Ophiocordyceps* spore, it becomes "zombified", causing it to leave its nest in order seek out a suitable, humid place, usually the underside of a leaf, to firmly clamp itself to with its mandibles. There, fungus will ultimately consume the still living ant as it matures and grows, eventually sprouting "fruiting bodies" from the dead ant's husk that ultimately rupture and release its spores.

For a short period in early spring, the Australian wattle does the same, however, this time with mammals …

Once a human or any other mammal inhales the wattle spore, it only takes a day or so for the infected to have an overwhelming urge to stumble away into the nearest forest and hug a tree with an almost unbreakable death grip. Predators that would otherwise attack seem able to sense the infection and stay well clear.

It amazes me that some people still refuse a simple
yearly vaccination that can stave off tragedy!

THE BILBY

On their own, they make charming house pets; cute, cuddly and placid, with just a hint of mischief thrown in for good measure. However, if more than four or five get together, they become hyper-aggressive, fearless and far more ravenous than any half-starved Alaskan wolf pack!

These pocket-sized marsupials are capable of bringing down and stripping to the bone even the largest of beasts! Not a bad effort for a creature no bigger than a small dog ...

They are only mildly venomous, but have numerous triangular, shark-like teeth that aren't apparent until they open their oversized, extendable jaws, which are capable of taking a 5 centimetre (2 inch) bite of flesh from their pray with ease.

*Diminutive but supreme hunters, endowed with keen
eyesight, sense of smell and large omnidirectional ears,
they can detect prey a kilometre or more away!*

THE BANDICOOT

The "randy" bandicoot has a similar attitude to life as the notorious bonobo monkey on a cocktail of steroids and viagra. No household pet or suburbanite is safe from the tenacious advances of this insatiable sex-crazed predator!

Though not dangerous to life and limb, the bandicoot's unquenchable sexual appetite is infamous, and a thoroughly unpleasant nuisance as they will launch themselves without warning on to any creature big or small and forcibly try to mate with them.

A simple trip to the shops or leisurely stroll around the neighbourhood can have you running a gauntlet of uninvited marsupial sexual advances!

Carrying a tennis racquet and being the possessor of a good backhand and forehand swing is usually not only effective, but a highly satisfying defence against an attacking bandicoot.

THE NUMBAT

For some strange reason best known to itself, and as of yet unexplained by naturalists and scientist alike, the numbat will aggressively attack and maul the "nether regions " of any male creature that ventures into its territory. Many a "naturist", as well as prize stud bulls, rams and stallions, has had promising careers cut short by the vicious attentions of the numbat!

*The notorious 1987 attack at the Whatalongdong
Private Naturist Retreat.*

THE FLYING FOX

Very alluring and even cute when they're little, they prefer to eat fruit and nuts. They eventually mature into a 90+ kilogram monster of the sky, and that's another story! This horror will attack day or night on silent, 2-metre wings, completely envelop its prey in them, and feed!

They also carry the potentially lethal lyssavirus and Hendra virus, but that's usually the very least of our problems. >>

THE BRUSHTAIL POSSUM

A marsupial nightmare found in most parts of Australia, and probably the vilest creature in the entire world, the bite of this possum causes total and permanent paralysis within 10 minutes!

Brushtail possums normally prefer to attack their victims while they are sleeping or otherwise vulnerable, but they also seem to enjoy stalking their prey silently through the trees or on the ground. They attack quickly and economically by leaping onto the victim, and administering two or three quick bites before scuttling away.

Only when the victim succumbs to the venom and is helpless (as well as still fully conscious) will the monster return to feast …

The only real defence is constant vigilance and a yearly vaccination.

A vile monster in every way!

THE QUOKKA

South America has the vampire bat, Australia has the dreaded quokka! The quokka is an antipodean "Nosferatu", and uses its cute and seemingly sweet nature to seduce and mesmerise its unwary victims into a false of sense security before gently sedating and killing them.

The saliva of the quokka is a remarkable chemical cocktail with the properties of a strong painkiller, topical anaesthetic, narcotic and sedative.

What seems like a friendly little lick followed by what appears to be a small painless love bite are in fact the precursor to a fatal attack in which the victim never really becomes aware they are slowly being killed.

The quokka then carefully and quietly drains every last drop of blood from the victim's body and strips them of their flesh, essentially nibbling them to death.

NEVER look into the eyes of a quokka, EVER!

THE WOMBAT

The mighty wombat can grow to about a metre and a half and can weigh as much as 800 to 900 kilograms. It has the similar unpleasant disposition to the African rhino — smelly, short-sighted, full of muscle and with a bad attitude!

When on the charge, the wombat can reach speeds of up to 75 kilometres/hour over short distances, and is capable of obliterating anyone unfortunate enough to get in its way! These dumb brutes of the bush have been known to pursue and trample mountain-bike riders and even upend small cars and SUVs!

They are prodigious tunnellers — an individual wombat tunnel can go for hundreds of metres, and if it joins up with another wombat's diggings, the tunnels can stretch for kilometres! It is a well-known fact that the Sydney railway tunnel system and other underground rail systems across Australia will often follow and enlarge upon pre-existing wombat diggings.

A little-known piece of recently declassified Australian martial history can now be found in the famous military textbook Jane's Weaponised Marsupials, which reports that specially trained wombats were deployed into the Vietcong tunnel systems causing terror and mayhem. Only a full clip fired from an AK-47 at point blank range could bring their subterranean rampage to an end!

Brace for impact!

THE RED KANGAROO

Red kangaroos, as well as most other larger roo and wallaby species, are well-known sexaholics of the bush. They are renowned and feared as aggressive and indiscriminate sexual predators of the worst possible kind as they will mate vigorously with anything, anywhere at any time.

Bushwalkers must be on their guard or become victims of marsupial carnal assault. Is it any wonder the females of the species (equally as sexually aggressive) are nearly always pregnant, with all manner of unpleasant things being found at the bottom of a kangaroo's pouch …

The word "kangaroo" is Aboriginal for "dirty old man". In fact, when Captain Cook pointed a finger at one of them and asked of a friendly local, "What is that odd creature over there?", the first Australian thought the good captain was making unsavoury advances towards him and told him so.

There are some deviates in our antipodean population, however, who find their solid, well-buffed bodies and instinctive flexing highly arousing, and will often claim that once you've "hopped in the pouch with a big red boomer, you'll never go back …"

Not my cup of Darjeeling, I can tell you!

THE PLATYPUS

The platypus is the mightiest of all the monotremes and the undisputed monarch of our inland waterways! Usually this titan is a solitary hunter of the streams and rivers, but during their breeding season, platypi will congregate in large numbers (called a "bask") where the "bull" males joust for dominance and the right to form and maintain a harem.

A big bull platypus can weigh in as much as 900 kilograms, and they have been known to drag full-grown scrub cattle into the water and strip their flesh down to nothing within a few bone-splintering minutes.

The platypi's armoury consists of:
- A broad and muscular bill full of short, strong teeth
- Webbed feet with long, razor-sharp claws
- A flat, strong tail that can be used for fighting as well as swimming
- A venomous, rapier-like barb on its hind legs that injects a poison lethal enough to kill a bull elephant
- A tough, thick hide that seems to be impervious to almost any attack.

The female of the species has all of the above but also lays eggs like a snake and then nurtures its young in a pouch once they hatch.

It is often said in Australia that if you ever wanted proof that God sometimes drinks or has a sense of humour, then the Platypus is it!

The platypus has been known to attack small
boats, kayaks and other watercraft, and a constant
lookout must be maintained at all times!

THE ECHIDNA

Slow with a clumsy waddling gate, no bigger than a house cat, and nowhere near as aggressive or spectacular as the mighty platypi, the echidna is nonetheless the most feared of all monotremes due to its highly unpleasant feeding and breeding habits.

The echidna is a stealthy and cautious predator that comes armed with an acute sense of smell and a fearsome array of sharp, toxic quills that it is capable of propelling to about 5 metres. The quills themselves are nonlethal, but the toxin they carry contains a remarkably strong anaesthetic that can sedate a victim for a day or more. After sedation, the echidna will then nonchalantly shamble up to its fallen prey and delicately chew a small hole through the victim's nasal passage or ear canal with its long snout. Once a sufficiently sized hole is dug, the echidna will then use its lengthy tongue to suck out the victim's nutrient-rich brain.

In the mating season, this habit changes, with the echidna carefully depositing a single small egg while leaving the brain intact. If the host regains consciousness, the mother will simply launch a few more quills to quiet them down again.

After a few days, the larval echidna (known as a "puggle") will hatch and chew its way out of the host, when it will then be transferred to the safety of the mother's pouch and remain there for several weeks until it is ready to fend for itself.

An echidna feeding on its victim's brain after sedation.

THE SUGAR GLIDER

Small, furry, mischievous and endearing, sugar gliders are as dangerous as they are sweet and delightfully cute!

Omnivores by nature and preferring the nectar of flowers as well as the odd grasshopper, they become voracious carnivores during the mating season, always on the hunt for easy prey and woe betide anyone blundering into their nesting sites during this time!

The alpha male or "bull" normally leads a typical sugar glider attack. Silently leaping out of the trees, the "bull" will cover the mouth and nose of the victim in the folds of its wings in an attempt to smother them. He is rapidly followed by his "harem", who swiftly glide down and latch on to the victim's body, securing any limbs so their prey is unable to move, run or defend themselves. Once this is done, there is little chance of escape, and the victim could be described as basically being "cuddled to death".

*What the sugar glider lacks in size and strength
it makes up for in numbers and aggression.*

TASMANIAN DEVIL

A denizen of the Tasmanian wilds, the "Tazzy" devil has a well-deserved reputation for its foul odour, bad temper and tenacious ferocity. Armed with a thick hide, an acute sense of smell and powerful bone-crushing jaws, they are fortunately no larger than a large house cat and have always preferred to steer clear of humans. As such, nasty encounters have been a rare occurrence ... until recently.

In the last few years, the beast has been plagued with a particularly horrid form of facial tumour disease that has decimated its population. As a side effect, Tasmanian devils have become hyper-aggressive, and will now wildly attack anything that approaches. Research to find a cure is underway and seems to be bearing fruit, for as unpleasant as the Tasmanian devil is, we would still hate to see it go extinct and pass into history forever.

Up close and personal with an infected Tasmanian devil!

THE KOALA

As agile as a gibbon in the trees and as fast as a greyhound on the ground, this iconic beast is the apex predator of the Australian continent and is a true monster in every possible way!

Even though they are very cute and cuddly when they're little, heavily sedated and with their venom glands removed, once they grow to their full 120+ kilogram size and start hunting for meat, that's a whole other story!

The koala is an active and aggressive hunter and possesses immensely strong front and hind claws, not only to cling to the trunks of trees, but to latch onto and hold fast to their prey. When hunting on the ground, they can put on a surprising burst of speed that can have them easily bring down scrub cattle or even a horse and rider!

The front teeth of the beast consist of two broad, flat, razor-sharp, chisel-like incisors capable of slicing off a full kilo of meat and bone with one bite!

Carnivores to the last, they have been known to attack and eat their own young. This is possibly why newborn cubs have a fast-acting, though comparatively weak venom that dissipates as they mature, along with their taste for eucalyptus leaves.

Though man is not their natural prey (feral pigs and goats being their favourite delicacies), they are opportunistic and indiscriminate killers and will attack almost anything that blunders into their territory. A single koala can claim up to 3 square kilometres of bushland as its own.

A little known fact (often ignored by most Australian historians) concerns our notorious bushranger Ned Kelly.

It seems Ned's lesser known brother Fred Kelly was actually killed and eaten by a bull koala, and that the Kelly gang's famous armour had little to do with thwarting police bullets, but was in fact the first early attempt at a defence against the tooth and talon of the fearsome koala (see the front cover)!

The nonsensical and imaginary "drop bear" is nowhere near as deadly as the real thing!

THE DINGO

Australia's native dog has had a bad rap over the years, with some very nasty and fatal attacks being recorded. Caution should always be exercised when in their territory for this reason. However, dingoes have also been known to take in lost children and other wanderers of the outback, raising and caring for them as if they were their own.

THE CANE TOAD

The cane toad was introduced from South America to Australia in 1935. This was done as a natural means of eradicating the native grey-backed cane beetle and French's beetle populations, which both enjoy feasting on Queensland's sugarcane crops.

Since that time, the toads have thrived, mutated and multiplied at an astonishing rate, without touching a single cane beetle, which they apparently find unpalatable. These toads instead enjoy eating just about everything else that crosses their path — big or small. If a toad thinks something will fit into its mouth, it considers it lunch.

Of course, this being Australia, the last home of mega-fauna, some cane toads have mutated to an alarming size ...

Upper picture: And it's only been a couple of days ...
Lower picture:A cane toad enjoying "lunch". >>

THE LAMINGTON

In closing, I must now draw attention to the sad tragedy of the once proud Australian lamington!

The lamington was a remarkably adaptive species and a wonder of the animal kingdom, able to withstand the rigours of the Australian continent in all its harsh diversity. From barren deserts, steaming tropical rainforests, frigid alpine rangers to deep rivers and coastal waters, the lamington held dominion over them all!

Many years ago, its vast majestic herds would stretch from horizon to horizon of our inland plains, and the seasonal joustings of their "Bulls" and "Bucks", accompanied by their mighty bellows and roars, were as loud as cannon fire. Their thundering migrations were dubbed the "Great Lamington Drive", and they were a thing of wonder to behold!

Alas, these times have long past, and the wild untamed lamington is no more, for over-hunting and a lack of respect for the environment has decimated this once proud species, leaving it now nothing more than a pathetic shadow of its former glory.

Gone are the Great Woolly and Sabre-toothed Lamingtons of the Ice Age. Gone are the Sure-footed Alpine Rock Lamingtons and the playful, water-loving lamingtons of the rivers, streams and billabongs. Gone is the majestic great Blue Lamington of the Southern Seas, and the packs of wild hunting lamingtons of the deserts and plains. All are now extinct, all are now gone and never to return.

From mighty, wild and free-ranging to stunted, industrialised and malformed; the "battery lamington", a national disgrace!

WARNING AND DISCLAIMER

While the Australian animals and flora written about and depicted in illustrations in this book are real, the dimensions, weight, height, attributes, characteristics (murderous, perverse, sexual or otherwise) and sizes are fictional and intended to be humorous, comical and farcical.

For example, red kangaroos are not really sexually interested in human beings, nor do they bound around with the intention of sexual assault. By way of further example, the pods of banksia trees are not explosive and have never been used as quasi hand grenades or otherwise as a weapon of war, calamity or terror.

However, in real life, the Australian flora and fauna depicted in this book in text or illustration can pose serious risk of severe injury or death if approached and handled. For example, the fictional character of "Harrold the Funnel-web Spider", as depicted in this book, does not wear a collar, but will inflict a potentially fatal bite upon anyone attempting to affix such attire to him, no matter how fetching it may be in appearance. Wasps sting, no matter where they are encountered.

Similarly, avoid any snake, wombat, kangaroo, spider, possum, shark, octopus, insect, bird or any other creature mentioned in this work in text, illustration or both, and any attempt to handle any Australian native fauna should be under the direct supervision of a suitably trained and qualified person. Be wary of the Australian native flora or introduced species of flora (such as lantana), and only handle the flora described in the text or illustrated in this book under the direct supervision of a suitably trained and qualified person.

The author, illustrator, distributor and publisher of this book accept no responsibility for any injury, loss or damage, howsoever occasioned, if a person were to attempt to imitate or mimic any of the fictional scenarios described in the text of this book or depicted in any illustrations contained in this book.

We do recommend that you try the lamingtons though. They are (and always have been) cakes. They are delicious. The lamington recipe was not pilfered from our wonderful neighbours from New Zealand.

Otherwise, I hope you enjoyed this light-hearted, ironic and farcical work.